NATIONAL GEOGRAPHIC

D0503654

# School Today and Long Ago

Mario Lucca

My great great grandpa lived a long time ago.
When he went to school,
he carried his book in his hand.

I carry my books in my bag.

When my great great grandpa went to school…

…his classroom looked like this.

This is my classroom.

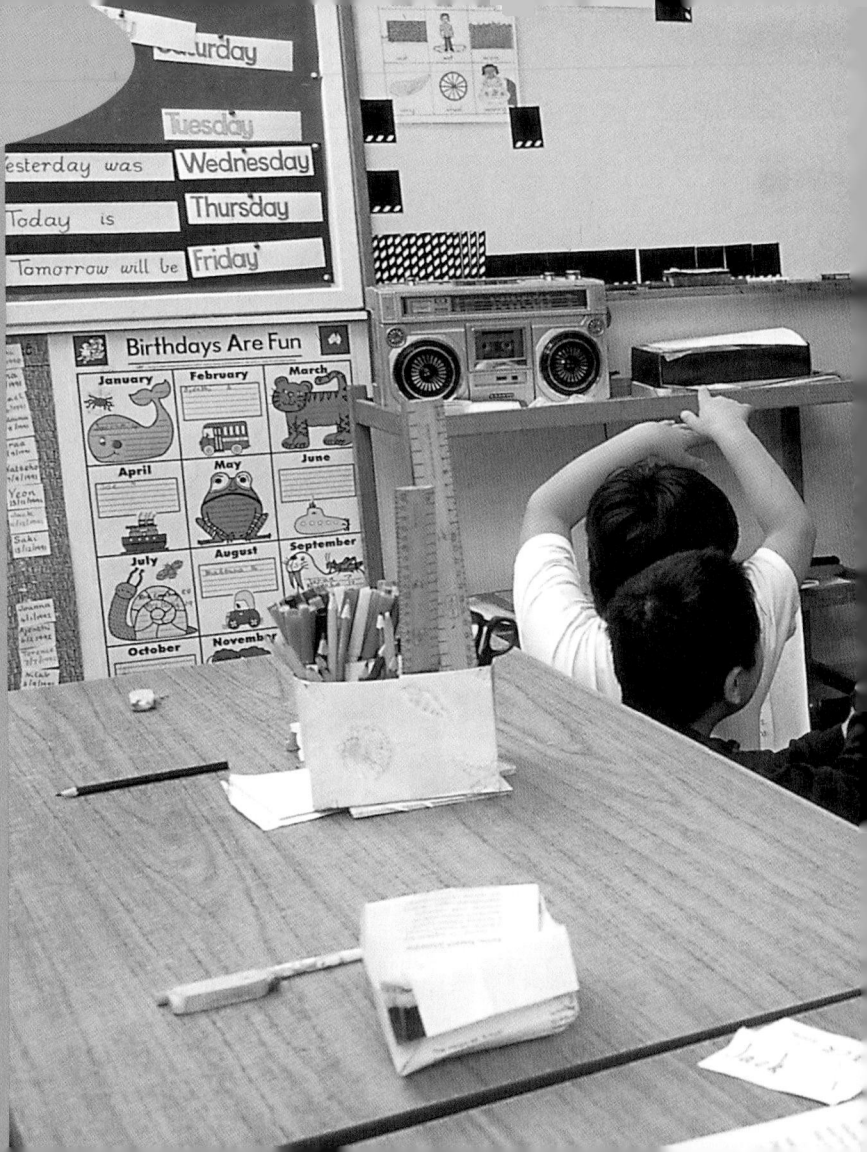

smells very beautiful
Write On!
1 one
2 two
3 three
4 four
5 five
6 six
7 seven
8 eight
9 nine
10 ten
11 eleven
12 twelve
13 thirteen
14 fourteen
15 fifteen
16 sixteen
17 seventeen
18 eighteen
19 nineteen
20 twenty
times table

When my great great grandpa went to school, he sat at a wooden desk.

I sit on a chair at my desk.

When my great great grandpa went to school,
he wrote with chalk.
He wrote on a slate.

I write with a pencil.
I write on paper.

When my great great grandpa went to school, he liked his teacher.
Friday May 8th
I have a fam
I have a
smells very beautiful
Thursday
Homes are built of many things
Geometric
I like my teacher, too.